THROUGHOUT THE DAY

MAGNIFICAT
BENEDICTUS
NUNC DIMITTIS

D1081752

O Lord, open my lips,
and my mouth shall declare your praise

The Sign of the Cross

In the name of the Father
and of the Son and of the Holy Spirit.

Psalm 63

God, my God, you I crave;
my soul thirsts for you,
my body aches for you
like a dry and weary land.
Let me gaze on you in your temple:
a vision of strength and glory.

Your love is better than life,
my speech is full of praise.
I give you a lifetime of worship,
my hands raised in your name.

I feast at a rich table,
my lips sing of your glory.

On my bed I lie awake,
your memory fills the night.
You have been my help,
I rejoice beneath your wings.
Yes, I cling to you,
your right hand holds me fast.

Let those who want me dead
end up deep in the grave!
They will die by the sword,
their bodies food for jackals.
But let the king find joy in God.
All who swear by truth be praised,
every lying mouth be shut.

More psalms are found on pages 6, 9 and 16.

The Canticle of Zechariah

Praise the Lord, the God of Israel,
who shepherds the people and sets them free.

God raises from David's house
a child with power to save.
Through the holy prophets
God promised in ages past
to save us from enemy hands,
from the grip of all who hate us.

The Lord favored our ancestors
recalling the sacred covenant,
the pledge to our ancestor Abraham,
to free us from our enemies,
so we might worship without fear
and be holy and just all our days.

And you, child, will be called
Prophet of the Most High,
for you will come to prepare
a pathway for the Lord
by teaching the people salvation
through forgiveness of their sin.

Out of God's deepest mercy
a dawn will come from on high,
light for those shadowed by death,
a guide for our feet on the way to peace.

Prayer for Others

Pray now for the world, the church, especially
your parish, your family and friends, and
your own needs. If you pray with others, after
each person speaks the intention, all may
say, *"Lord, hear our prayer."*

The Lord's Prayer

Our Father . . .

EVENING PRAYER

O God, come to my assistance.
O Lord, make haste to help me.

The Lighting of a Candle

Jesus Christ is the light of the world,
a light no darkness can overcome.

See also the prayer on page 60.

Psalm 141:1–5, 8

Hurry, Lord! I call and call!
Listen! I plead with you.
Let my prayer rise like incense,
my upraised hands,
   like an evening sacrifice.

Lord, guard my lips,
watch my every word.
Let me never speak evil
or consider hateful deeds,
let me never join the wicked
to eat their lavish meals.

If the just correct me,
I take their rebuke as kindness,
but the unction of the wicked

will never touch my head.
I pray and pray
against their hateful ways.

Lord my God, I turn to you,
in you I find safety.
Do not strip me of life.

More psalms are found on page 2, 9 and 16.

The Canticle of Mary

I acclaim the greatness of the Lord,
I delight in God my savior,
who regarded my humble state.
Truly from this day on
all ages will call me blest.

For God, wonderful in power,
has used that strength for me.
Holy the name of the Lord!
whose mercy embraces the faithful,
one generation to the next.

The mighty arm of God
scatters the proud in their conceit,
pulls tyrants from their thrones,
and raises up the humble.
The Lord fills the starving
and lets the rich go hungry.

God rescues lowly Israel,
recalling the promise of mercy,
the promise made to our ancestors,
to Abraham's heirs for ever.

Prayers for Others

Pray now for the world, the church, especially
your parish, your family and friends, and
your own needs. If you pray with others, after
each person speaks the intention, all may say,
"Lord, hear our prayer."

The Lord's Prayer

Our Father . . .

NIGHT PRAYER

**May Almighty God give us a restful
night and a peaceful death.**

Psalm 131

Lord, I am not proud,
holding my head too high,
reaching beyond my grasp.

No, I am calm and tranquil
like a weaned child
resting in its mother's arms:
my whole being at rest.

Let Israel rest in the Lord,
now and for ever.

The Canticle of Simeon

Lord, let your servant
now die in peacc,
for you kept your promise.

With my own eyes
I see the salvation
you prepared for all peoples:

a light of revelation for the Gentiles
and glory to your people Israel.

Invocation to Mary

Hail, holy Queen, Mother of mercy,
     our life, our sweetness, and our hope!
To you we cry, the children of Eve;
to you we send up our sighs,
mourning and weeping in this land of exile.
Turn, then, most gracious advocate,
     your eyes of mercy toward us;
lead us home at last
and show us the blessed fruit of your womb,
     Jesus:
O clement, O loving, O sweet Virgin Mary!

The Sign of the Cross

On Aging in Wisdom and Grace

Approaching Old Age

I must not disguise from myself the truth, I am definitely approaching old age. My mind resents this and almost rebels, for I still feel so young, eager, agile, and alert. But one look at my mirror disillusions me. This is the season of maturity; I must do more and better; reflecting that perhaps the time still granted me for living is brief, and that I am drawing near to the gates of eternity. This thought caused Hezekiah to turn to the wall and weep. I do not weep.

No, I do not weep, and I do not even desire to live my life over again, so as to do better. I entrust to the Lord's mercy whatever I have done, badly or less than well, and I look to the future, brief or long as it may be here below, because I want to make it holy and a source of holiness to others.

— *Pope John* XXIII

In Our Dreams

One thing I've noticed since I got this old is that I have started to dream in color. I'll remember that someone was wearing a red dress or a pink sweater, something like that. I also dream more than I used to, and when I wake up I feel tired. I'll say to Bessie, "I sure am tired this morning. I was teaching all night in my dreams!"

Bessie was always the big dreamer. She was always talking about what she dreamed the night before. She has this same dream over and over again, about a party she went to on Cotton Street in Raleigh, way back when. Nothing special happens; she just keeps dreaming she's there. In our dreams, we are always young.

—*Sadie Delany*

Lord of Our Growing Years

Lord of our growing years, with us from infancy,
Laughter and quick-dried tears, freshness and
    energy:
  Your grace surrounds us all our days,
  For all your gifts we bring you praise.

Lord of our strongest years, stretching our
    youthful pow'rs,
Lovers and pioneers, when all the earth seems
    ours:
  Your grace surrounds us all our days,
  For all your gifts we bring you praise.

Lord of our middle years, Giver of steadfastness,
Courage that perseveres, when there is small
    success:
  Your grace surrounds us all our days,
  For all your gifts we bring you praise.

Lord of our older years, steep though the road
    may be,

Rid us of foolish fears, bring us serenity:
   Your grace surrounds us all our days,
   For all your gifts we bring you praise.

Lord of our closing years, always your promise
      stands;
Hold us when death appears, safely within your
      hands:
   Your grace surrounds us all our days,
   For all your gifts we bring you praise.

—*David Mowbray*

The Crown of Age

How attractive is sound judgment in the
      gray-haired,
   and for the aged to possess good counsel!
How attractive is wisdom in the aged,
   and understanding and counsel
      in the venerable!
Rich experience is the crown of the aged,
   and their boast is the fear of the LORD.

—*Sirach 25:3–6*

Like a Single Day

*A human lifetime is only a moment. A brave
prayer not only for mercy but for the gift of joy.*

You have been our haven, Lord,
from generation to generation.
Before the mountains existed,
before the earth was born,
from age to age you are God.

You return us to dust,
children of earth back to earth.
For in your eyes a thousand years
are like a single day:
they pass with the swiftness of sleep.

You sweep away the years
as sleep passes at dawn,
like grass that springs up in the day
and is withered by evening.

For we perish at your wrath,
your anger strikes terror.
You lay bare our sins

in the piercing light of your presence.
All our days wither beneath your glance,
our lives vanish like a breath.

Our life is a mere seventy years,
eighty with good health,
and all it gives us
is toil and distress;
then the thread breaks
and we are gone.

Who can know the force of your anger?
Your fury matches our fear.
Teach us to make use of our days
and bring wisdom to our hearts.

How long, O Lord, before you return?
Pity your servants,
shine your love on us each dawn,
and gladden all our days.

Balance our past sorrows
with present joys
and let your servants, young and old,
see the splendor of your work.

Let your loveliness shine on us,
and bless the work we do,
bless the work of our hands.

—*Psalm 90*

Lord of All Hopefulness

Lord of all hopefulness, Lord of all joy,
Whose trust, ever child-like, no cares can destroy,
Be there at our waking, and give us, we pray,
Your bliss in our hearts, Lord,
at the break of the day.

Lord of all eagerness, Lord of all faith,
Whose strong hands were skilled
     at the plane and the lathe,
Be there at our labors and give us, we pray,
Your strength in our hearts, Lord,
     at the noon of the day.

Lord of all kindliness, Lord of all grace,
Your hands swift to welcome,
     your arms to embrace,

Be there at our homing, and give us, we pray,
Your love in our hearts, Lord,
    at the eve of the day.

Lord of all gentleness, Lord of all calm,
Whose voice is contentment,
    whose presence is balm,
Be there at our sleeping, and give us we pray,
Your peace in our hearts, Lord,
    at the end of the day.

— *Jan Struther*

I Get the Blues Sometimes

Now, honey, I get the blues sometimes. It's a
shock to me, to be this old. Sometimes, when
I realize that I am 101 years old, it hits me right
between the eyes. I say, "Oh Lord, how did this
happen?" Turning 100 was the worst birthday
of my life. I wouldn't wish it on my worst enemy.
Turning 101 was not so bad. Once you're past
the century mark, it's just not as shocking.

— *Bessie Delany*

Living in Light

Holy, holy God, sinless and living in light,
God at whose bidding all things move as you
think it best for them; whose blessing falls
on those who love you enough to trust you
utterly: my soul praises you with the energy
it draws from the Spirit; my heart praises you,
Lord, and would praise your power unceasingly;
the whole of my being praises you, Lord,
because if you will it so, God, I shall be yours.

God of the poor, helper of the insignificant,
you watch over the humble and aid the weak.
Help me then, Lord, since your grace has made
me pleasing to you. Let me be your servant,
since you let me bear the great name of
Christian. If you freed me from slavery, it was to
give me the chance of serving God the Most
High for ever, of singing the praises of the one
who sees everything.

Give us back our youth and enable us to build up your holy church, O Son, the Father's Word and Understanding.

O Christ, you came to save the human race; you died, were buried and rose again; you received glory from the One who sent you. Turn then, and help us, Lord. May we think the thoughts that we ought to think, guided by faith made strong by the Spirit. For our hope is in your Father and you and in the Holy Spirit, as it always will be, throughout the unending succession of ages. Amen.

— *The Widows' Prayer at Night, 4th century*

Big Things, Small Ways

In spite of illness, in spite of the archenemy sorrow, one can remain alive long past the usual date of disintegration if one is unafraid of change, insatiable in intellectual curiosity, interested in big things, and happy in small ways.

— *Edith Wharton*

Abraham and Sarah Advanced in Age

The LORD appeared to Abraham by the oaks of Mamre, as he sat at the entrance of his tent in the heat of the day. He looked up and saw three men standing near him. When he saw them, he ran from the tent entrance to meet them, and bowed down to the ground. He said, "My lord, if I find favor with you, do not pass by your servant. Let a little water be brought, and wash your feet, and rest yourselves under the tree. Let me bring a little bread, that you may refresh yourselves, and after that you may pass on— since you have come to your servant."

So they said "Do as you have said." And Abraham hastened into the tent to Sarah, and said, "Make ready quickly three measures of choice flour, knead it, and make cakes." Abraham ran to the herd, and took a calf, tender and good, and gave it to the servant, who hastened to prepare it. Then he took curds and milk and the calf that he had prepared, and set it before them; and he stood by them under the tree while they ate.

They said to him, "Where is your wife Sarah?" And he said, "There, in the tent." Then one said, "I will surely return to you in due season, and your wife Sarah will have a son." And Sarah was listening at the tent entrance behind him. Now Abraham and Sarah were old, advanced in age; it had ceased to be with Sarah after the manner of women. So Sarah laughed to herself, saying "After I have grown old, and my husband is old, shall I have pleasure?"

— *Genesis 18:1 – 12*

Only One Solution

There is only one solution if old age is not to be an absurd parody of our former life, and that is to go on pursuing ends that give existence meaning: devotion to individuals, groups or causes, social, political, intellectual or creative work.

— *Simone de Beauvoir*

Serenity Prayer

God grant me the serenity to accept the things I
    cannot change;
    courage to change the things that I can,
    and wisdom to know the difference.
    Living one day at a time;
    enjoying one moment at a time;
    accepting hardship as the pathway to peace;
    taking, as Christ did, this sinful world as it is,
    not as I would have it;
    trusting that Christ will make all things right,
    if I surrender to his will;
    that I may be reasonably happy in this life
    and supremely happy with him forever in the
       next. Amen.

ON AGING IN BODY

To Give Up and To Struggle

There's a few things I've had to give up. I gave up driving a while back—in my eighties. That was terrible. Another thing I gave up was cutting back my trees so we have a view of the New York City skyline to the south. Until I was 98 years old, I would climb up on the ladder and saw those tree branches off so we had a view. I could do it perfectly well; why pay somebody to do it? Then Sadie talked some sense into me, and I gave up doing it.

Some days I feel as old as Moses and other days I feel like a young girl. I tell you what: I have only a little bit of arthritis in my pinky finger, and my eyes aren't bad, so I know I could still be practicing dentistry. But it's hard being old, because you can't always do what you want, exactly as you want it done. When you get as old as we are, you have to struggle to hang onto your freedom, your independence.

—*Bessie Delany*

Bear Me Away with You

Grant, O God, when my hour comes, that I may recognize you under the species of each alien or hostile force that seems bent upon destroying or uprooting me. When the signs of age begin to mark my body (and still more when they touch my mind); when the ill that is to diminish me or carry me off strikes from without or is born within me; when the painful moment comes in which I suddenly awaken to the fact that I am ill or growing old; and above all at that last moment when I feel I am losing hold of myself and am absolutely passive in the hands of the great unknown forces that have formed me; in all those dark moments, O God, grant that I may understand that it is you who are painfully parting the fibers of my being in order to penetrate to the very marrow of my substance and bear me away within yourself.

— *Pierre Teilhard de Chardin, sj*

Blessing for a Cane

Like a watchful Shepherd
you care for us, O God,
your love a sturdy staff to support us.
Bless this cane that I now need
 to steady myself.
Make it strong to ease standing and sitting
 and a sturdy companion in walking.
As the serpent-staff that Moses lifted high
 in the desert
 healed the people of their afflictions,
 so may this cane bring me,
 if not healed hips and strengthened knees,
 peace of mind and a more steady standing.
Blessed are you, good Shepherd, now and
 forever!

Blessing for a Wheelchair

God of earth and heaven,
 the prophet Elijah ascended to your throne
 in a chariot whose wheels were wind
 turned by horses of fire.

Bless this wheelchair that I now need
    to move about.
Make it my chariot of charity
    that in it I may draw nearer to you
    and bring the good news of your love
    to all that I meet.
Legs, knees and hips may fail us,
    but you are faithful forever.
Blessed are you, God of earth and heaven!

And God Gave Skill

The Lord created medicines out of the earth,
    and the sensible will not despise them.
Was not water made sweet with a tree
    that its power might be known?
And God gave skill to human beings
    that he might be glorified in marvelous works.
By them the physician heals and takes away pain;
    the pharmacist makes a mixture from them.
God's work will never be finished;
    and from God health spreads
    over all the earth.

—*Sirach 38:4 – 8*

Living God,
   when you spoke, all things came to be
   and from prophets' mouths
      Israel heard your word.
   You sent Jesus to open the ears of the deaf:
   With a touch and a word
      your holy Name echoed
   in ears that had been dead.
Bless this hearing aid that I now need.
May it amplify life clearly for me:
   With those who laugh
      may I give you praise
   with those who cry may I beg your help
   and in the noise of this world
      as well as its silences
   may I always hear your voice.
Blessed are you, the God who speaks to us, now
      and forever!

NEW BEGINNINGS

ABRAHAM
SARAH

Abram Went as God Told Him

Now the LORD said to Abram, "Go from your country and your kindred and your father's house to the land that I will show you. I will make of you a great nation, and I will bless you, and make your name great, so that you will be a blessing. I will bless those who bless you, and the one who curses you I will curse; and in you all the families of the earth shall be blessed."

So Abram went, as the LORD had told him; and Lot went with him. Abram was seventy-five years old when he departed from Haran.

—*Genesis 12:1–4*

My Tower of Strength

Lord, you are my shelter,
do not fail me.
You always do right;
deliver me, rescue me,
hear me and save me.

Be my rock and haven,
to whom I can always turn;
be my tower of strength,
keep me safe.
The ruthless and wicked trap me;
reach out to free me.

You are my hope, O Lord,
from the days of my youth.
I have relied on you since birth,
my strength from my mother's womb;
I will praise you always.

I am shunned like the plague,
but you keep me in your care.
I am filled with your praises,
all day I sing your glory.
Now I am old, my strength fails,
do not toss me aside.

From childhood till now
you taught me to praise your wonders.
Do not leave me, Lord,
now that I am old.

I can still recount
to a new generation
your power and strength.
Your goodness is boundless,
your works so great;
who can equal you?

You wrack me with torment,
but you give back my life
and raise me from this grave.
You will restore my honor
and wrap me again in mercy.

I will thank you, Lord,
for your true friendship
and play the lyre and harp for you,
the Holy One of Israel.
I will sing out with joy,
sing of how you saved me.

— *Psalm 71:1–9, 17–23*

The Old Man Taught

It is said that once upon a time the people of
a remote mountain village used to sacrifice and
eat their old men. A day came when there was
not a single old man left, and the traditions were
lost. They wanted to build a great house for
the meetings of the assembly, but when they came
to look at the tree-trunks that had been cut for
that purpose, no one could tell the top from the
bottom: If the timber were placed the wrong
way up, it would set off a series of disasters.
A young man said that if they promised never
to eat the old men any more, he would be able
to find a solution. They promised. He brought
his grandfather, whom he had hidden; and
the old man taught the community to tell top
from bottom.

— *An old Balinese tale*

The word of the LORD came to Abram in a vision, "Do not be afraid, Abram, I am your shield; your reward shall be very great." And the LORD brought him outside and said, "Look toward heaven and count the stars, if you are able to count them. So shall your descendants be." And Abram believed the LORD; and the LORD reckoned it to him as righteousness. As the sun was going down, a deep sleep fell upon Abram, and a deep and terrifying darkness descended upon him. Then the LORD said to Abram, "As for yourself, you shall go to your ancestors in peace; you shall be buried in good old age." On that day the LORD made a covenant with Abram, saying, "To your descendants I give this land."

—*Genesis 15: 1, 5, 6, 12, 15, 18*

FOR OTHERS

Prayer for All Needs

We beg you, Lord,
to help and defend us.

Deliver the oppressed.
Pity the insignificant.
Raise the fallen.
Show yourself to the needy.
Heal the sick.
Bring back those of your people
    who have gone astray.
Feed the hungry.
Lift up the weak.
Take off the prisoners' chains.

May every nation come to know
that you alone are God,
that Jesus is your Child,
that we are your people,
    the sheep that you pasture.
Amen.

— *St. Clement of Rome*

Prayers of Petition

Give peace to the nations of the world:
    Lord, have mercy!

Give wisdom to our pope, _____,
    our bishop, _____,
    and our pastor, _____ :
       Lord, have mercy!

Give enthusiasm and strength to
    all ministers of the gospel:
    Lord, have mercy!

Give joy to those who sorrow:
    Lord, have mercy!
Give shelter to the homeless
    and food to the hungry:
    Lord, have mercy!
Give comfort and help to the sick:
    Lord, have mercy!
Give rest to those who have died:
    Lord, have mercy!

For Young People

God,
we pray for our young people,
growing up in an unsteady and confusing world.

Show them that your ways give more life
    than the ways of the world,
and that following you is better
    than chasing after selfish goals.

Help them to take failure,
not as a measure of their worth,
but as a chance for a new start.

Give them strength to hold their faith in you,
and to keep alive their joy in your creation.

We ask this through Christ our Lord.
Amen.

For Friends in Nursing Homes

Lord Jesus Christ,
hope of the frail and the infirm,
remember Simeon and Anna,
the aged prophets who longed to see your face
and held you as an infant
brought to the Temple in your mother's arms.
Come today to comfort and redeem
my ailing friends in nursing homes,
especially _____
together with all those
   who devote nights and days
to serve them in their needs.
Give us all the grace to see your face
in one another
in peace and joy. Amen.

Give Graciously

Stretch out your hand to the poor,
  so that your blessing may be complete.
Give graciously to all the living;
  do not withhold kindness even from the dead.
Do not avoid those who weep,
  but mourn with those who mourn.
Do not hesitate to visit the sick,
  because for such deeds you will be loved.
In all that you do, remember the end of your life,
  and then you will never sin.

  —*Sirach 7:32–36*

On the PROMISE of the FUTURE

Abraham Laughed

God said to Abraham, "As for Sarai your wife, you shall not call her Sarai, but Sarah shall be her name. I will bless her, and moreover I will give you a son by her. I will bless her, and she will give rise to nations; kings of peoples shall come from her." Then Abraham fell on his face and laughed, and said to himself, "Can a child be born to a man who is a hundred years old? Can Sarah, who is ninety years old, bear a child?"

— Genesis 17:15 – 17

Moving with Wonder

Through our actions, we will create a new image of age—free and joyous, living with pain, saying what we really think and feel at last—knowing more than we ever knew we knew, not afraid of what anyone thinks of us anymore, moving with wonder into that unknown future we have helped shape for the generations coming after us.

— Betty Friedan

These Are the Days

Listen! I will be honest with you,
I do not offer the old smooth prizes, but offer
     rough new prizes.
These are the days that must happen to you.
You shall not heap up what is call'd riches,
You shall scatter with lavish hand all that you
     earn or achieve,
You but arrive at the city to which you were
     destin'd,
   you hardly settle yourself to satisfaction before
   you are call'd by an irresistible call to depart,
You shall be treated with ironical smiles and
   mockings of those who remain behind you,
What beckonings of love you receive you shall
     only
   answer with passionate kisses of parting.
You shall not allow the hold of those who spread
     their
   reach'd hands toward you.

— *Walt Whitman*

I find myself remembering. And that, some tell us, is a disease of the graying and the balding. To go back is to bore, to praise the "good old days." To remember is to bask in the past, to enter an Eden that never existed, a paradise as legendary as Atlantis. To remember is to start dying.

But no, 'tis not so; quite the opposite. I recall Abraham Joshua Heschel's startling affirmation: Much of what the Bible demands can be summed up in a single word—Remember! I discover in ancient Israel a community of faith vitalized by memory, a people that knew God by reflecting not on the mysteries of nature but on its own history. . . . And Elie Wiesel, that remarkable Jewish storyteller who feels guilty because he survived the Holocaust, has reminded us that, for Jews, to forget is a crime against justice and memory. If you forget, you become the executioner's accomplice.

Importantly, Johannes Metz has distinguished our memories. There are memories that simply make us feel good, because they glide over all that is oppressive and demanding. And there are memories that are dangerous, because they make demands on us, reveal perilous insights for today, illuminate harshly the questionable nature of things with which we have come to terms.

The most demanding type of memory for the Christian? The passion, death, and resurrection of Jesus Christ. In this context, to remember is to start living.

— *Walter J. Burghardt, SJ*

As Evening Falls

Give me more light as evening falls. O Lord,
we are now in the evening of our life. I am in my
seventy-sixth year. Life is a great gift from our
heavenly Father! Three-quarters of my contem-
poraries have passed over to the far shore. So
I too must always be ready for the great moment.
The thought of death does not alarm me. Now
one of my five brothers also has gone before
me — my beloved Giovanni. Ah, what a good life
and a fine death! My health is excellent and
still robust, but I cannot count on it. I want to
hold myself ready to reply *adsum* at any, even
the most unexpected moment.

Old age, likewise a great gift of the Lord's,
must be for me a source of tranquil inner joy,
and a reason for trusting day by day in the Lord,
to whom I am now turned as a child turns to
his father's open arms.

— *Cardinal Roncalli, one year before he was elected
Pope John XXIII*

November

The trees are getting bare, but still it stays warm. The warm sweet smell of the good earth enwraps one like a garment. There is the smell of rotting apples; of alfalfa in the barn; burning leaves; of wood fires in the house; of pickled green tomatoes and baked beans.

There is the warm feeling of contentment about the farm these days—the first summer is over, many people have been cared for here. This month of Thanksgiving will indeed be one of gratitude to God. For health, for work to do, for the opportunities to be of service, we are deeply grateful, and it makes the heart swell with joy.

We can be thankful for the trials of the past, the blessings of the present, and be heartily ready at the same time to embrace with joy any troubles the future may bring us.

—*Dorothy Day*

Out of Her Poverty

Jesus sat down opposite the treasury, and watched
the crowd putting money into the treasury.
Many rich people put in large sums. A poor
widow came and put in two small copper coins,
which are worth a penny. Then he called his
disciples and said to them, "Truly I tell you, this
poor widow has put in more than all those
who are contributing to the treasury. For all of
them have contributed out of their abundance;
but she out of her poverty has put in everything
she had, all she had to live on."

— *Mark 12:41 – 44*

ON LOSING A CHILD OR A SPOUSE

MARY

JESUS

His Mother's Only Son

Jesus went to a town called Nain, and his disciples and a large crowd went with him. As he approached the gate of the town, a man who had died was being carried out. He was his mother's only son, and she was a widow; and with her was a large crowd from the town. When the Lord saw her, he had compassion for her and said to her, "Do not weep." Then he came forward and touched the bier, and the bearers stood still. And he said, "Young man, I say to you, rise!" The dead man sat up and began to speak, and Jesus gave him to his mother.

—Luke 7:11–15

Abraham Wept for Her

Sarah lived 127 years; this was the length of Sarah's life. And Sarah died at Kiriatharba (that is, Hebron) in the land of Canaan; and Abraham went in to mourn for Sarah and to weep for her.

—Genesis 23:1–2

Buried with His Wife Sarah

This is the length of Abraham's life, 175 years.
Abraham breathed his last and died in a good
old age, an old man and full of years, and was
gathered to his people. His sons Isaac and
Ishmael buried him in the cave of Machpelah, in
the field of Ephron son of Zohar the Hittite,
east of Mamre, the field that Abraham purchased
from the Hittites. There Abraham was buried,
with his wife Sarah.

— *Genesis 25:7–10*

Prayer of One Who Has Lost a Spouse

Holy God,
I thank you for married life
that I shared with my spouse.
Not all our days were even:
Some brought pain,
    some were filled with joy.
And now I mourn as I remain alone.

Grant eternal peace to _____.
   Forgive and heal the hurts
   that troubled us at times.
Bless the good that we accomplished together
   that it may live on in all who knew us.
And send an angel of peace
   to soothe my sorrow
   in the name of Jesus the Lord. Amen.

Love Each and Every Day

Over the years, we've buried a lot of people. Even the generation younger than us is starting to die off. I don't know why I'm still here and they're not, but I don't fret over it.

You know, when you are this old, you don't know if you're going to wake up in the morning. But I don't worry about dying, and neither does Bessie. We are at peace. You do kind of wonder, when's it going to happen? That's why you learn to love each and every day, child.

—*Sadie Delany*

Where You Die, I Will Die

[After her husband and two sons had died, Naomi] set out from the place where she had been living, she and her two daughters-in-law, and they went on their way to go back to the land of Judah. But Naomi said to her daughters-in-law, "Go back each of you to your mother's house. May the LORD deal kindly with you, as you have dealt with the dead and with me." Then she kissed them, and they wept aloud.

Orpah kissed her mother-in-law, but Ruth clung to her. So Naomi said, "See, your sister-in-law has gone back to her people and to her gods; return after your sister-in-law."

But Ruth said, "Do not press me to leave you or turn back from following you! Where you go, I will go; where you lodge, I will lodge; your people shall be my people, and your God my God. Where you die, I will die—there will I be buried. May the LORD do thus and so to me, and more as well, if even death parts me from you!"

—Ruth 1:7 – 8, 9b, 14 – 17

Lament of One Who Has Lost a Child

How can this be, my God,
   that I must now bury my child?
Tell me how. Tell me why.
Was it not my own child who would wrap my
   body in a shroud and bear it to the grave?
Yet now death has taken my own from me!
My heart is broken concrete, jagged in my chest;
   my tears are acid in my eyes.
Grief bends my back;
   sorrow shatters my soul.
How can I hold my grief? Answer me.

   O Mother of Jesus,
   at Golgotha you felt his pain;
   your arms received his broken body.
   Pray for us in our sorrowful days!

FOR A HAPPY DEATH

The Meeting

Now there was a man in Jerusalem whose name was Simeon; this man was righteous and devout, looking forward to the consolation of Israel, and the Holy Spirit rested on him. It had been revealed to him by the Holy Spirit that he would not see death before he had seen the Lord's Messiah. Guided by the Spirit, Simeon came into the temple; and when Mary and Joseph brought in the child Jesus, to do for him what was customary under the law, Simeon took him in his arms and praised God, saying,

"Master, now you are dismissing
    your servant in peace,
  according to your word;
for my own eyes have seen your salvation,
  which you have prepared
    in the presence of all peoples,
a light for the revelation to the Gentiles
  and for glory to your people, Israel."

There was also a prophet, Anna the daughter of Phanuel, of the tribe of Asher. She was of a great age, having lived with her husband seven years after her marriage, then as a widow to the age of eighty-four. She never left the temple but worshiped there with fasting and prayer night and day. At that moment she came, and began to praise God and to speak about the child to all who were looking for the redemption of Jerusalem.

—*Luke 2:25 – 32, 36 – 38*

Holy Rest and Peace

May God support us all the day long till the shades lengthen and the evening come and the busy world is hushed and the fever of life is over and our work is done. Then in mercy may God give us a safe lodging and a holy rest and peace at the last.

—*John Henry Newman*

The Evening Has Come

We thank you, O God,
through your Child, Jesus Christ our Lord,
because you have enlightened us and revealed to
    us the light that is incorruptible.
The day's allotted span is over;
    we have reached the beginning of the night.
We have had our fill of the daylight
    which you have created for our pleasure.
And now that the evening has come
    and again we have no lack of light,
we praise your holiness and your glory
    through your only Son, our Lord Jesus Christ.
Through him the glory and power that are his
    and the honor that is the Holy Spirit's
    are also yours, as they will be
    throughout the unending succession of ages.
    Amen.

— *The Apostolic Tradition of Hippolytus*

An Act of Communion

You are the irresistible and vivifying force,
O Lord, and because yours is the energy,
because, of the two of us, you are infinitely the
stronger, it is on you that falls the part of
consuming me in the union that should weld us
together. Vouchsafe, therefore, something more
precious still than the grace for which all the
faithful pray. It is not enough that I should die
communicating. Teach me to treat my death as
an act of communion.

— *Pierre Teilhard de Chardin, SJ*

Acknowledgments *continued*

Quotes from *The Divine Milieu* by Pierre Teilhard de Chardin.
Copyright © 1957 by Editions du Seuill, Paris. English
translation copyright © 1960 by Wm. Collins Sons & Co.,
London, and Harper & Row Publishers, Inc., New York.
Renewed © 1988 by Harper & Row Publishers, Inc. Reprinted
by permission of HarperCollins Publishers, Inc.

"Blessing for a Cane," "Blessing for a Wheelchair," "Blessing
for a Hearing Aid," "For Friends in Nursing Homes," "Prayer
of One Who Lost a Spouse," "Lament of One Who Has Lost
a Child" written by David Philippart.

An old Balinese tale (p. 35) is from *Aging* by Henri J.M.
Nouwen and Walter J. Gaffney. Copyright © 1974 by Henri
J.M. Nouwen and Walter J. Gaffney. Used by permission
of Doubleday, a division of Bantam Doubleday Dell Publishing
Group, Inc., New York.

Excerpt from "Song of the Open Road," by Walt Whitman,
from *Walt Whitman: The Complete Poems,* edited by Francis
Murphy. New York: Penguin, 1975.

Quote by Dorothy Day from *Dorothy Day: Selected Writings,*
edited by Robert Ellsberg. Maryknoll, New York: Orbis Books,
1992. Copyright © 1983, 1992 by Robert Ellsberg and Tamar
Hennessey. Used by permission of Orbis Books.

"Lord of Our Growing Years," by David Mowbray, copyright
© 1982, Hope Publishing Company, Carol Stream, IL 60188.
All rights reserved. Used by permission.

"Lord of All Hopefulness," by Jan Struther, copyright © 1931,
from *Enlarged Songs of Praise,* used by permission of Oxford
University Press.

"The Widow's Prayer at Night" and "We thank you, O God
through your Child," from the book *Early Christian Prayers*
translated by Walter Mitchell. Copyright © 1961 by Regnery
Publishing, Inc. All rights reserved. Reprinted by special
permission of Regnery Publishing, Inc., Washington, D.C.

Quotes from Betty Friedan, Edith Wharton and Simone de
Beauvoir ("There is only one . . .") taken from Helen Nearing,
ed., *Light on Aging and Dying,* Gardiner ME: Tilbury House
Publishers. Text copyrighted by Helen Nearing, 1995.